MW00463840

Girl Talk

The Transgender Guide for Voice and Feminization

Lynette Nisbet, M.S.

Girl Talk

© 2012 Lynette Nisbet

ISBN: 978-1-61170-077-0

All rights reserved. No part of this publication may be reproduced, stored in a retrieval system or transmitted in any form or by any means, electronic, mechanical, photocopies, recording or otherwise, without the prior written consent of the author.

Printed in the USA and UK on acid-free paper.

Robertson Publishing™
59 North Santa Cruz Avenue
Los Gatos, California 95030 USA
www.RobertsonPublishing.com

This book has been created following the compilation of 22 videos, PDFs and exercises from my on-line program which can be found at *MyFemVoice.com*.

It is intended to lay out for you, the step-by-step how-to's on discovering your feminine voice, attitude and appearance.

I encourage you to go to the website and see the program. You just can't beat the repetition of live demonstrations, examples, exercises and accessing me as your personal coach!

I want you to have fun, try it, laugh, build your confidence and above all, be yourself!

TABLE OF CONTENTS

There is only one success - to be able to spend your life in your own way.

~ Christopher Morley

INTRODUCTION

I'm Lynette and I've been practicing as a Speech Pathologist since 1993. I completed my M.S. and life hasn't been the same since!

After years of working in the hospital, doing home health, holding a position as a Rehabilitation Director, I was burnt out on the usual grind. I wanted to do something new.

I moved to the city of Chicago and decided I would open my own voice practice, working with actors, T.V. talent and general voice-over talent. I had loads of fun with my clients. They were animated, happy and hungry for success.

One afternoon, I received a call from Jan (not my client's real name). She told me that she was mid-transition from male to female. She wondered if I could help her with her voice, hmmm, I wondered.

I told her that I would have to get back to her as I had to take a look at my materials and see if I could effectively work with her. I looked at my books, notes and tossed them aside. The conversation went something like this....

"Hi, Jan?"

"Yes."

"I looked through my materials. As far as I can see anatomy for the voice and neck haven't changed since I left college. I know quite a bit about working with voice and have some ideas. I'm up for giving this a go if you'd like. I'm pretty sure we can do it."

"Fantastic! Thursday at 4:00?"

"Perfect!"

And that's how it started. Jan, the lawyer, arrived to my home office and we started. A few weeks later, she was ready to present herself as a female litigator.

What a change and how quickly! This was amazing.

Soon after Jan, my name started to circulate in the TG, MTF community and I had many clients. Many that I have helped not just with their voices but with their overall presentation of their "femaleness", if you will.

It became about helping in a complete real, functional way, as in, "I really need to look, sound and become, totally and completely, a woman." The word of choice was..."*passable*."

This is how I have come to help...voice, shopping, girl-friend, appearance, behavior... all of it. It is a package.

This book is offered to help in several ways. It is meant to help start you on the right track to sounding more feminine and understanding some of the basic characteristics that most or many women have and how to apply these to yourself.

Take it in, absorb the information, use it and call or email me at the end. I am, after all, Your Fem Voice Coach.

Have patience with all things, but chiefly have patience with yourself. Do not lose courage in considering your own imperfections but instantly set about remedying them – every day begin the task anew.

~ Saint Francis de Sales

BREATH SUPPORT

Alright, this is the main crux of learning where your power comes from. Your volume, the nice flow and the nice even keel of your voice is all dependent on your breath support. You get your power from your breath, your lungs.

Where your diaphragm sits, is right, kind of at the meeting point where your rib cage is. So if you just put your hand on your diaphragm and feel where that is right now, you'll get the idea. That muscle is dome shaped. What happens when you breathe in, is that it flattens out, so it goes down. That gives you more space in your chest cavity to actually have power and support. The air, which is going to go up through your pharynx, through your larynx, comes out of your mouth eventually and becomes your voice when you speak. This is otherwise known as phonation. So, phonation, all that means is, making sound, that is coming through your vocal folds.

To build this power here, in your core, is kind of like every Pilates or Yoga class you've seen. It's the core. Everybody's interested in the "core". The downside is that everybody is taught to walk around feeling really tense and hard in this area. For our purposes, I don't actually want you to be tense and hard. I want you to be relaxed and I want you to be natural. I don't want you to feel like it's a "six pack" competition. I want you to keep relaxed in the area as we're going to work through it.

The first thing I want you to do is a little exercise. I'm going to ask you to just take a deep breath. So go ahead and just take a deep breath. Ok good, I'm sure you took one. And as you're doing that, I'm sure your shoulders went up and sky high! It happens every time. These shoulders, when you take a deep breath, should not rise up because you're not breathing with your shoulders. You're actually not getting any power by lifting them up. You're just adding tension. You're adding additional flexion you don't need. And that is going to go through into your neck, affect your voice and you're going to get tight. Tightness is definitely what you don't want!

So the first exercise here is being able to put your hand on your own stomach, and when you breathe, your stomach would actually go out a bit. You'll feel that as it rises and falls. If you're lying down it's really easy to see. That's a natural position that will allow you to experience the sensation. I know it's different and employs different muscles but it is a useful tool for you to experience the sensation of the outward movement in the area of your diaphragm. The point here is to establish a power source and omit tension all together.

Now, put your hand on your stomach and take a nice deep breath in through your nose or your mouth or whatever's comfortable. You can feel your stomach rise out just a little bit and when you exhale, it goes back down. There should be no action occurring in your shoulders or neck. It should be nice and loose. Usually I would be standing in front of you and if you would need some additional coaching, we could work that out. Just keep your shoulders down.

Get in front of the mirror and just practice in and out breathing. Just natural breathing. You do it all day long. You do it all the time. Somehow it becomes a confusion when you start doing these drills. I'm just trying to bring you back to the natural motion of the body. It truly is what you do and you do it all day long.

When you go to practice, stay loose and keep the shoulders loose. You want to keep them down and not raised. You want your stomach pretty relaxed. You want some motion there. You're not trying to hold everything in tight, in your back and in your butt and your hips; you want to keep this generally loose.

A good analogy of how *not* to do this would be trying to walk like a toy soldier. Everything is really stiff and tightened up. That posture would affect the diaphragm and everything up through your chest, your neck, your larynx and pharynx. No creating tension!

So the area from the hips up should be minimal tension. I do want you to be able to stand with nice posture; but without tension. Keep it nice and loose.

This is going to help optimize your breath support for a good, strong, fluent, relaxed voice. Later on you will be able to overcome, in different social settings or crowded places like shopping malls, restaurants or what have you, being able to comfortably talk in a loud enough voice by keeping this tension out.

I'm going to say it again. Practice keeping your shoulders down. Keep your shoulders nice and loose. You just shake them out and check in the mirror if you must, but *know* that they are down and relaxed.

There are some other things you can do. Roll your neck if you feel like it's really tight. Look left and right over your shoulders to stretch out the muscles. Go up the street; pay $120 for a ½ hour of pure pleasure...

the Deep Massage. I'm pretty sure you won't be able to stand nor will you care that your shoulders are up or down because now, you will be drooling with relaxation. The more exercise, the more fit you are all together, the better you're going to be in position for almost anything. It's the same thing for your voice.

When you take a deep breath, you can feel it all expand through your chest cavity and you'll feel your ribs actually expand. Then, you'll feel your ribcage contract back in. This is because, this is the cavity that it's filling. It's not your shoulders or your neck. It's nowhere else but the chest cavity.

That's really it in a nutshell. Practice this over and over and look at yourself over and over. Get in the mirror and look and see if you're feeling or seeing tension as you're doing it. You can even touch your own neck. Double check it by raising them up to your ears and then dropping them. You're ready to go!

If you don't like something, change it.
If you can't change it, change your attitude.

~ Maya Angelou

Vocal Hygiene

Every time I start with a new client, we go over some basic things. This is so she is aware of the very basic underlying information that needs to be in place for consistently handling and working with the voice.

The first four things we go over are:
1) Hydration
2) Relax
3) Rest
4) Proper Use of Your Voice

The first thing we want to address is hydration. All of us love coffee. All of us love tea. All of us love wine. All of us love beer. All these things, however, are diuretics and pull moisture from your body. So if you want to keep your body hydrated and your vocal folds moist, (which is important for learning how to properly use your voice, we'll talk about that in a little bit) you want to make sure that for almost every cup of coffee or cup of tea that you have, you're going to have a glass of water to go with that. It's kind of an "8 ounce rule". Whatever caffeine or diuretic type of thing you might be drinking, water should also be a part of the intake.

Typically, I also hear recommendations for drinking lemon juice or juices; but there's a lot of citric acid in those things. If you put the lemon peel or juice on your hands, it pulls things out, cleans your skin amazingly, even gets ink off! But it totally dries out your skin. If you remember Madge from the old Palmolive commercial, whose hands were soaking in dish soap, the hands dry out with the lemon extract and so will your vocal folds. It treats your voice the same way, so it can act very dehydrating to your body and you'll get a lot of throat clearing when you're practicing and a lot of different effects you necessarily don't want nor are they good for your voice overall.

Make sure that when you are working on your voice, one of the first things you're doing is hydrating properly.

The second thing I want to mention is rest. If you are tired, it's not a good time for you to practice. If you're voice sounds groggy, if your voice sounds crackly, if your voice sounds raspy and you think you're sounding like Demi Moore after a long day of phone calls and talking, (it might be sexy, it might be nice sounding to you at the moment), it's actually *not* the time for you to sit down and practice your voice and your pitch exercises.

If you're tired and your body feels tired then muscles throughout your entire body, including your chest, neck and pharyngeal area, are also compromised and fatigued. They're not exempt from any other fatigue that you'd be feeling.

So make sure when you're working on your voice, you are actually rested when you're practicing. It's a new activity for you and you are definitely working on increasing your awareness of your pharyngeal and laryngeal areas as well as the overall position of your body.

The next thing I want to talk to you about is just simply relax. When you're first learning to use your voice and first starting to practice, I know there is a lot of anxiety. Most of us carry it through the back of our necks, shoulders and generally throughout our body. We're always rolling our heads and trying to relax and lift our shoulders. There are actually some exercises you can do that can help prepare you and loosen you up so that you can maximize your voice and your practice. In doing so you won't get additional tension in your neck and in your shoulders and in your back and all these places that actually affect your voice.

Your voice is a unit and a tool within your body. It's not in and of itself, alone. You can't work on it by itself. It is affected by so many other things. The tension and the things that will be impacting your voice, your practices, your pitch and all the things that you're trying to optimize, will do much better if you just remember to relax and keep those muscles all relaxed. This will really help when you're learning these new motions and positions, e.g. how to carry yourself, use your voice, female mannerisms, etc...

The fourth and last point is pretty all encompassing. It's using your voice properly. I know that sounds ridiculous but I know you have witnessed abuse, including hearing people screaming, cheering, yelling over crowds, using a high pitched falsetto, which means they're not using the actual vocal folds at all.

Not using the actual vocal folds that you should be using is misuse and potentially abuse over time. We don't want to abuse the voice. We don't want to give you little calluses on your vocal folds. Nodules are what they are called. Many singers get these. I mean, Steven Tyler is probably "heroic" in the nodule department. Elton John has had them several times. Lots of singers get these from the stress on a specific area of their vocal folds so we want to minimize any chance for that occurring with you.

When you are able to relax, omit tension and consistently have good breath support, you will optimize your vocal production. You can have a really nice sounding voice, with a clear, comfortable pitch without putting stress on your voice. It kind of all comes together with proper use.

So, stay well rested. It's good for you anyway. Keep a good amount of hydration in your body. That's also good for you. If you're drinking a lot of coffee or a lot of tea or things that are going to pull out any excess hydration, then you want to make sure you are *re*hydrating your body. And you want to make sure that you're not tired or super fatigued or sore or aching. You don't want to end up pushing and putting too much extra effort on your voice when you're trying to learn something that is actually quite natural and which you already have within yourself. We're actually just going to find it, pull it out and give you your tool to use, in its best form. Amen!

One of the things I learned the hard way was that it doesn't pay to get discouraged. Keeping busy and making optimism a way of life can restore your faith in yourself.

~ Lucille Ball

THE VOLUME OF YOUR VOICE

This is the chapter that explains where you are really going to get your power.

You've already read the chapter on breath support, and this is what is going to influence the volume. So, if needed, refer back to the chapter "Breath Support" and you'll understand why it comes from the core, why we do not want to have tension and why you should keep your shoulders down. Make sure you've practiced in the mirror and make sure that you're overall relaxed when you're getting ready to do this.

I know that when you go out and you're dressed, looking gorgeous; you're nervous and you have this anxiety happening. I want you to be able to *keep it together*. And it's important that you keep it together. Keep your confidence up on what you have learned about your voice. When you keep it together, you're going to stay relaxed and then you will have a nice stable, lovely sounding voice. So let's just work on the basics of volume.

We've gone over putting your hand on your stomach and making sure you're getting a good, deep breath. You're not walking around taking deep breaths every time you're speaking (that would be really bizarre to look at somebody do that). Air naturally, by the course of physics alone, flows from high to low pressure. When you inhale, the diaphragm contracts and thus expands the chest cavity. Due to the expansion, the pressure lowers in the chest cavity and the air pressure externally is higher. This is how the air flows naturally in and out of the lungs. So every time your body runs out, you automatically get this little "fill up". You don't have to have attention on taking air in and worrying about your breathing.

You have to make sure you're not talking too long on one breath. If you're talking, blah, blah, blah, and you run out of breath and you start to feel the effort which changes in your diaphragm and neck and starts to push through, you can feel the tension start to build up. So when you're running out of air, take another breath and keep talking. You'll keep stability and a comfort level within your voice.

I'm going to go back over that again because this is where you don't want to get into misuse of your voice and you want to keep a nice, stable sound.

When you start running out of air (using up your reserve) and you "aaaaah" hold it out and then you start to push and you just *have* to get one more word before somebody's gonna talk over you… you're way past the point of any optimum voice function. You don't want to go past that point. It would be similar to the sensation of being under water too long, not sure if you'll resurface fast enough to take a breath and you begin to feel the pressure.

This is something I've found, truth be told, in families with a lot of kids. If you grew up in a family with a lot of kids, people are talking until they have run out of air totally. They are getting that last mashed potato or getting that last muffin, and they just don't care about their voice. They care about the muffin, right? It becomes a "voices competing" kind of thing. But it becomes misuse and abuse over time.

You have to retrain that behavior, should it be a habit. Misuse or abuse can, potentially, create nodules, which are little calluses or little polyps on the vocal folds. If you've ever had a blister on your foot from wearing new shoes, this would be similar to a polyp. It's friction in a place where friction does not belong.

We're trying to prevent and eliminate any voice problems or misuse. Don't talk to the end of your breath. That is the main point of that!

The second part is once you've refilled, and you're ready to start talking, make sure you're talking at the top of your breath; that you're not just letting all of the air go out and then start talking because you got nervous. You don't want to take a breath and go (air let out) "So now I'm going to tell you about..."

You're already out at that point! You've already let a good amount of your support go. So you talk on the top of your breath. You take it in and you start to talk on the top of it until you start to feel a tiny effort and then you go back and you have to refill. This happens naturally... most of the time.

Don't keep going just because you're afraid you can't get your pitch back. You will always get your pitch back because we're going to train you on how to get your pitch and maintain it. This part of support right now is just on volume, attention on the loudness, because if you have enough power and have full breath support, you can go from controlling how soft you want to talk or just decide to talk loud and you're not using any more effort.

If you have enough support, it will naturally push through the exact amount of energy with the exact amount of effort that you want to have at the time. Your voice will remain fine, constant and clear. Straining, harshness and breaks in pitch will all fall away.

Now, as far as being in competing noise situations, where you're going to have to drag up the volume on your voice quite a bit and you're maybe not that comfortable...all you have to really remember is your power comes from your diaphragm, the core area. If you take a good breath, have good support, right in your diaphragm, right under that bra-line, you're going to be fine and you can keep your voice up.

There is a difference that is noteworthy between men and women regarding when they raise the volume of their voice. When men yell, their voices go down. It's this low kind of gravelly, fighting voice. But when women raise their volume, their pitch goes way up!

When you get into a louder situation and you need to compensate for the difference in volume, you should hear your voice going up and not down.

To do this you need good breath support. Having the correct support will enable you to fully let that voice out, just the way you want it to. Just like you've been practicing keeping your pitch up, when you're yelling in a crowd or you're shouting or you're screaming at a concert or you're simply in a restaurant ordering where there's a lot of noise, keep the breath support going and don't drop back down in pitch. I've seen that happen plenty of times when I've been out with my clients.

Make a conscious effort to keep it up. If there's music in the background, if there are waitresses, if there are people talking all around you, just keep the pitch up and you'll do fine.

Of course I am not promoting vocal abuse or screaming or yelling or anything of the sort. However, I would be remiss to think that this situation would never occur!

20 years from now you will be more disappointed by the things that you didn't do than by the one's you did do. So throw off the bow lines. Sail away from the safe harbor. Catch the trade winds in your sails. Explore. Dream. Discover.

~ Mark Twain

THE TRUTH ABOUT YOUR VOICE

Now I'm going to tell you the truth about your voice. And the reason I'm calling it "The Truth About Your Voice" is because it really is so unique to you. When you actually develop the voice you're looking for, the feminine voice you're after, it depends on so many different things.

What I don't want you to have is a standard that is going to be unreachable or a have goal that you simply can't attain. So I'm going to tell you about some things that you may have heard about, read about, seen from other videos or seen from other clips from voice coaches, speech therapists, whoever... but let's really just look at the simple truth of who you are physically, concurrently with what your voice is going to sound like.

You've got all these structures that are going to influence the sound of your voice. It is simply not what's happening in your larynx (or Adam's apple). It's actually consistent with your sinus cavity, how much air is able to go back and forth inside or resonate against that, the thickness of your muscle in your chest cavity, your cheeks, chin, tongue, teeth, tonsils, soft palate, hard palate... all of these articulators. The air passes through these things before you get any sound emitted from your mouth. Your head, your face, your nose, your throat, this whole area called your pharynx, ok? And then of course the kind of breath support you've got and what you're able to get as far as power and support from that. So all of these things influence naturally and the things we can't see (unless under a scope), like the size of your vocal folds, how thick or how thin they are.

All of those things are such dimensions and anchor points to what you can actually go for, that's going to create the sound for the ideal voice for you. The goal is not to sound like somebody else or have a voice like somebody else. Because I know we all want to look a certain way or we've all been to the hairdresser and we all want Jennifer Aniston's hair and we want it to be just so. I once saw a sign and it read, "You know, I'm a beautician, not a magician." Right? So, that kind of rings true for what you have to work with. Everybody doesn't have the same hair. Everybody doesn't have the same voice or the same set of vocal folds or the same structures to pass through.

I understand or rumor had it, that at one point, Barbara Streisand entertained the idea of having rhinoplasty (a nose job). However, rumor also had it, that she decided not to, due to the fact that the surgery could significantly change the resonance of her voice….thus change her career. I suppose the aesthetic quality to her voice outweighed that of her nose. I agree! She is one of the best, female vocalists I know.

I want you to know that you have a voice that is going to sound right for you. I don't know how familiar any of you are with Lauren Bacall but she's got an extremely low voice for a woman. Oprah Winfrey actually has a pretty low voice for a woman as well. You can come up with several examples if you just look around. It's not just how low or high your voice is. We'll go into the exercises that are going to lead into why a woman's voice sounds like a woman. It's not just based on the pitch.

Also keep in mind that after you have surgeries, particularly nasal surgery, if you're having nose work done, or any kind of dental work or shaping, it will change the resonance and voice sound as well, inadvertently. You're not going to have control over that. So, if you've been working on your voice, and then you have surgery, that could shift. And you should be aware of that.

Additionally, if you are intubated during the surgery, which means that a tube is place down your throat between your vocal folds to provide oxygen and anesthetic gases, this may have some effects on your voice following surgery. The surgeons can provide information on this to you.

When intubated, your voice may not return for a couple of days, give or take a day. This is fairly usual. I just wanted to give you a little bit of that information that you can use, so that you know where the influences are coming from and how to work within that.

All of these structures and factors influence your voice. This information is useful so that you're not setting goals that are unattainable during your transition or during your practicing.

You will be able to attain a feminine quality regardless of different physical structures. It is a package.

We'll, go into the exercises later to "find your voice". But for now, I wanted to tell you about... the *truth* of your voice.

I like looking feminine and I enjoy being a role model. I enjoy being a woman. It all comes down to having the confidence to be who you are.

~ Cathy Freeman

How To Find Your Pitch

This is the chapter I know everybody's been waiting for. But let's go over a few things first.

What is pitch? Per the Wikipedia definition, pitch can be defined as "an auditory perceptual property that allows the ordering of sounds on a frequency-related scale. Pitches are compared as "higher" and "lower" in the sense associated with musical melodies, which require "sound whose frequency is clear and stable enough to be heard as not noise. Pitch is a major auditory attribute of musical tones, along with duration, loudness, and timbre.

Pitch may be quantified as a frequency, but pitch is not a purely objective physical property; it is a subjective psychoacoustical attribute of sound."

Wow, what a mouthful! Let's simplify it a bit. Pitch is basically how high or how low your voice is. This depends upon frequency of vibrations and the musical quality to the voice that is perceived by listening. Everybody has a natural range in their pitch.

In order for us to find your feminine voice and your pitch that best suits you and create that in a comfortable range, there are a few things to do. We went over the breath support and vocal hygiene and now we're ready to begin to discover your pitch.

Remember, it's important for you to find your pitch so it represents you, it's comfortable, you're not abusing your voice and it's pretty easy to do.

Ok, so this is the diagram. I want you to get some pa-per....yup, paper and pencil. We're going to draw this. I've used this forever and it's conceptually pretty easy to understand.

I want you to draw a vertical line nearly the length of the paper. This line that you've just drawn is a represen-tation of your vocal range, ok? We'll call it that... "vocal range."

Now draw a horizontal line at the top and one at the bottom. It should look like this below.

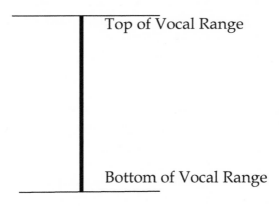

So, there is a low point to your voice and there's also a high point to your voice.

What I would like you to do is say "ah" just like you're at the doctor's office, nice and easy does it. (Now I'm sounding like Frank Sinatra). I want the sound to be easy and natural.

From that relaxed "ah" I want you to say eight (8) sep-arate notes or sounds higher from where you started. This is an octave. Do not glide the sounds connected-ly up or put them together. I'd like you to make eight (8) distinct, separate sounds. When you've done this, mark them with tally marks on the paper. It should look something like this below.

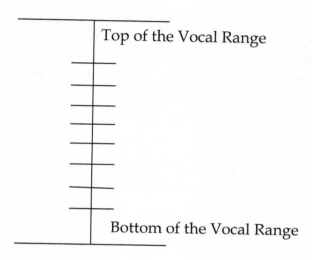

If you are able to do more than eight notes, great! Mark all of the sounds that you are able to make.

Start again at your usual or habitual pitch, "ah", and see how many notes you can go below your usual pitch.

The tally marks will go above or below the note that you started with, depending upon the note being higher or lower. Simply tally above or below where you started. The higher you can go, the more tally marks that will appear. And the lower you can go beneath your usual, habitual pitch, (the main voice you speak in all of the time), mark them at the bottom of the vocal range picture.

Your pitch is in that range; between the low and the high on the vocal range chart. Once you've found where you comfortably speak, as a male, go up about four to six notes and your new feminine pitch should reside there.

This is an approximation of where and how to find your new voice.

Take your voice and we're going to start at the bottom and we'll go "ah, ah, ah, ah, ah, ah, ah, ah" (on a rise). No falsetto. I want you to use your actual voice. We are not singing. We're speaking. No need at all for falsetto. Falsetto sounds funny, doesn't use the true vocal folds and can be damaging over time so we don't want to use that.

About here, is typically where you'll find the range for the feminine voice (See diagram).

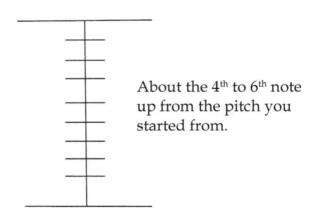

About the 4th to 6th note up from the pitch you started from.

Out of all the people that I've worked with, this is where you'll find it, about four to six notes up from the original speaking voice.

Find the bottom of your voice or your usual speaking voice and say, "ah". It's not going to sound harsh or raspy or gravelly; it's going to have a nice, clear sound.

Next, go up to the note (4th, 5th, 6th or otherwise) and hold that note out. See if that is the sound you are looking for.

Record yourself at that new sound and see how you like it. Voice is subjective, meaning that the way you hear it is not the way others perceive it. Using an outside means of hearing your voice will give you a more accurate perception.

This is due to the resonators in your body. You will hear your voice differently than others hear it. We want to ensure that you have a nice, feminine sound. We'll get the attributes to the feminine voice later. For now, just find the pitch that sounds pleasing.

Once you've found the note, turn your voice on and off to see that you can get it each time. This can be practiced and drilled so that you can easily get to your voice over and over.

Initially you can turn your voice on and off at the new pitch. Let's say 5 times to start. Begin with a short break in between turning the voice on and off. Gradually increase the time "off" and try again to hit your new pitch.

Move the number of times up to 10 and do the same thing. Again, gradually increasing the amount of time "off" so that you can practice just hitting the new pitch... bulls eye!

This should not be effortful at all! It is part of your usual range. There is no "push" on that pitch at all.

Now, back to the diagram for a minute. Take a look. The new note that you are using and have discovered to be your new pitch IS the new bottom of your voice. Get that? All of the tally marks below can now be just scribbled off. They are no longer part of your repertoire of sound when you speak. This is as simple as I can state this without working with you directly. The lower end of your "old" voice has disappeared. We're sending it on permanent vacation. All gone!

You'll *create* the flexibility in your voice by going up in pitch. So that new pitch being your new base or bottom sound will start to vary higher and be more flexible in *that* range. That's really what you're going for.

I would highly recommend purchasing the on-line program at *MyFemVoice.com* as a start. There are at least 4 four specific videos dedicated to this chapter. With audio and visual support, live demonstrations, examples and exercises your will definitely be in a much better place than before you started. The up-side is that you can review these over and over.

If needed, personal coaching and or review of the program will be available. Email me if you're having difficulty and we can set up a coaching session either live or by phone...we'll see.

In summary, this is the tool that I use and have been successful with in helping others find their new pitch. It's a starting point. It's what we want established so that we can move on to the other, eventually, conversational information.

If you get stuck, email me at lynette@myfemvoice.com. I will definitely be there to help you as Your Fem Voice Coach!

*A bad habit never disappears miraculously;
it's an undo-it-yourself project.*

~ Abigail Van Buren

The Vocal Warm-Up

This is the sequence of actions, a **real** sequence you take when you begin to practice your new pitch and voice. It is the proper gradient that allows you to move forward in a way that will stabilize your new voice and give you the confidence needed. This is all done so that you can have you use your voice everywhere in every situation, without hesitation. So let's get started!

1. Go back to the beginning and make sure that you're relaxed. Check for tension in your shoulders, neck and make sure you're not holding your body really rigid. Relax and keep everything loose when you're doing this. Loosy-goosy and keep it light.

2. The next thing that we're going to do is a little technique called the "Yawn-Sigh" (reference _The Voice and Voice Therapy_ 3rd Edition by Daniel R. Boone, copyright 1983). This is something pretty common in the speech world and it goes like this...

   Take a deep breath and as you're exhaling make a light sigh sound. This is very relaxed. It is for an easy onset of voice. If you're not sure you're doing it, put your hand on your neck and you'll feel your vocal folds in action; your vocal folds vibrating. You'll know that you are turning your voice on; you don't even have to worry about listening at that point. That technique opens up and relaxes this whole area (pharyngeal and laryngeal) in your neck.

3. What we're going to go for now is working a little bit with the scale. To start, keep all eight notes (the

octave) together and go up from your usual speaking voice. I'll refer to this as "gliding." We're not going to chop it up or separate the notes just yet.

You're going to do the scale, using your new pitch you found earlier and take it from the bottom of your voice up to the top of your voice. Use the "ah" sound since this is very easy and relaxed.

Once you've got that and it feels smooth, no pitch breaks, which means a crack or momentary shut-off in your voice, you can begin to slide your voice like a trombone. If it shuts off or cracks, no good, too much tension; you have to loosen up. Go back to loosening up and do the Yawn-Sign again until you have a nice relaxed sound.

Ok, so you're going to go up and down. Clarifying further, it really is like a trombone. Slide or glide your voice up and then back down again, stopping at your new pitch. It's the new base, remember? You can practice this as often as you want.

4. Next you're going to separate the sounds by turning your voice on and off in between each note or sound, again using "ah". It's almost staccato, but not quite. Also use the starting point of your new pitch to do this exercise. Go up the octave or more if you can do it, keeping the voice smooth, clear and effortless. This will really help you establish control of your pitch.

The off and on of your voice with the steps in between is really a solid way to begin working at the muscle memory.

5. It's time to use vowels. Let's stick with "ah" or "oh"

because those are nice, open, easy sounds that do not require added tension and do not constrict the pharyngeal or laryngeal area.

Repeat the above procedure with gliding the vowel sounds and then separating them.

6. Time to practice with single syllable words. I've listed some examples for you below:

Hi	Bed
Here	Car
Chair	See
House	Hot
Live	Tell

The first word is "hi". Say it 10 times in your new pitch (it's the note you found earlier, 4th, 5th, etc). Let's make sure you can get that word, 10 times, not changing pitch, but keeping it at your new pitch.

Then go to the next word. Turn your voice on and off for that and then you'll go to the next word. Complete the list of words and you'll move onto the next step.

7. The next point is significant and is a definite point to distinguish male and female voices. It is the variation of pitch in words.

Women actually vary their pitch quite a bit; on one word and on one syllable. On one of the YouTube videos I put out, the voice tip was about single syllable elongation. The demonstration was with "Hi". It's just a greeting, but women go "Hiiiii" (varied pitch, gliding like the trombone) and they go through this scale and they say "It's miiiiiine" (varied pitch) and it goes through a scale. And, "Come over heeeeeeere". It doesn't sound the same all the time and there is definitely length added to that single syllable word and there is definitely a variation in pitch. It is dynamic. Here's the link if you'd like to view the video:

www.youtube.com/watch?v=pY1wrXN-vSg

When you walk into your house at night or you walk to work and you're passing and you say "hey" or "hi". The male response would be "hey, hi, yeah" (flat, monotone and staccato). Women, for example say, "Oh yeeeeaaah", "Yes, I DID see that!" and they'll be speaking in these little, short but elongated phrases. There's emotion tied to this short little thing and it just drags out these syllables.

Really, this is a key component and a key part of getting your voice changed over so that you have the variation in the pitch. Somebody who has a lower voice and is female doesn't necessarily sound male because the pitch is so much lower. She sounds female because she's varying her pitch. ("Oh, yeaaaaaaaaah, I read that book!"), and she brings it up at the end and there's a rise in tone. The trick is to not to go too far off into the "valley girl" sound.

It is the same with questions. If a guy asks you a question, for example, "You get the milk? Did ya bring it home?" (flat, monotone and staccato). It's just this flat, drop off, blah, blah. It doesn't sound very romantic, friendly or anything like that for the most part. The women will come in and they're a little bit tentative, they don't want to upset somebody, and they're saying, "Hi, did you get the milk???" (varied pitch). Like, "just a reminder... want to make sure you didn't forget it..." It's not nasty or hostile or covert. It's just, mostly, the way women do it.

This pitch variation is really something to work with. You have the single words and then you're going to go on to your sentences, which are also provided here. Don't forget on the questions to lilt the sound up a bit at the end. I'm going to mix these up for you.

- Did you make it on time?

- Go over to the counter.

- Let me have your phone number please.

- I'd like to order the chicken marsala.

- Do you have change for a $20.00?

- I have so many emails to answer.

- I'll be a bit late tonight.

- I'm happy to let you borrow it.

- Did you see that movie?

- I'd love to go on a cruise!

8. Finally you're going to go onto some simple paragraphs. I didn't write out the paragraphs. This is what I'm going to tell you to do. Go get the Cosmo, the People magazine, Reader's Digest, I actually don't care which one...Outdoors, Adventures, any catalog, the Victoria's Secret, whatever. You can read anything in there. Read about sizes of clothes and colors and foo foo this and that. It doesn't really

matter. But in doing your reading, make sure that you are varying your pitch. "Wow that is a size extra small. I cannot believe that this extra small comes in a zero to a size 2. Who can wear that?" (Sorry, humor me please. You've seen what I'm talking about!)

You're going to vary it through that simple reading. It's just an exercise to do so that you have something that you can pick up at any time, read, and practice.

Feel free to start later in the warm-up if you've got several steps down. Perhaps you start at the sentences or the reading. It's your call. Just make sure you have *really* got the voice down solidly.

You'll graduate to leaving your home and going out and having conversations. Certainly, feel free to try that at any time.

I want you to feel comfortable and start using your voice in life!

Be a good listener.
Your ears will never get you in trouble.

~ Frank Tyger

Auditory Training

This is the mainstay of vocal training. Auditory Training is being able to hear the differences in your own voice. The goal with this is to be able to differentiate when your voice sounds good and when it's, aaaah, not so good. There's so much technology out there and so many tools you can use to record yourselves and play yourselves back that you should ensure you have a reliable tool to use.

Your best tool is actually your ears. The idea through this training is to get you to "listen" and get you to be able to become your own coach. If you can use your ears as your own feedback, eventually, this is, really, the most reliable source that you have. You will be able to use your own ears to "tune your instrument", that is, your voice. If you can't recognize what sounds good or what doesn't sound good, then it doesn't really matter and the lot of it becomes fairly pointless.

Being able to spot your pitch by means of some tool, that can give you a little bit of feedback, until you're good at saying "yes, that's my note" or "that's the sound I'm after" is great. But eventually you'll need to depend on your ears and that is optimum.

Also, I don't want you to hang up on just "a sound". What makes a man sound like a man and a woman sound like a woman depends upon many factors. Not just one; not just the amount of vibration in the vocal folds. So don't get hung up on *a* sound. Your ability to hear the pitch you're looking for, train your ears into just finding that pitch and then being able to work with it, move it around, assimilate it, is going to give you the feminine quality that you're looking for.

What is most beautiful in virile men is something feminine; what is most beautiful in feminine women is something masculine.

~ Susan Sontag

WHY WOMEN SOUND LIKE WOMEN

This is the chapter where you find out why women's voices are so different from men and why a woman's voice sounds like a woman. It is NOT just in the pitch. It's in the characteristics of voice.

PITCH VARIATION

First, women vary their pitch. It changes all the time. It is not monotonous. It is not a flat sound. It moves around. It goes up and down. It is a dynamic entity! Generally speaking, men sound monotonous and a bit flat. This is not totally true with every male, but the general male voice is a flat, flat, flat, general, yeah, yeah, "I'm takin' the garbage... yeah", "Yup, I liked that dinner... it was good..." There's very little emotion in the voice. So number one is the pitch variation

ELONGATION OF SYLLABLES

Women hold out the syllables of words...elongate the syllables, stretch them out. The quality of making single syllable words turn into mulit-syllabic words. So the word "hi" can sound like four syllables, like "hiiiiiiiiii..." It's almost 4 different sounds after that elongation. It's not chopped off or staccato sounding...at all!

COMPLIMENT TO ESTABLISH REALITY

There is a feminine quality that is admired by many. It is how a woman will talk to just about anyone about anything!

Women, particularly girlfriends, often begin a conversation with a compliment. For example, "Cute top!" "Nice shoes." "Like your pants!" "Where'd you get your hair done?" "Gosh, that make-up is so pretty." "Did you go shopping?" "I like your bracelet." Anything that is complimentary and kind brings in this reality. It's like a club. It's like a Women's Club, on the planet. And it's something that is very real and it's engaging to women everywhere. You could be anywhere…give a compliment to somebody and that will engage them right away. They are feeling befriended by that. They enjoy it. It is a greeting. It is something nice to introduce yourself with. They pay attention; you're paid attention to and it's because you are caring about somebody else.

I'm not suggesting that you overwhelm every person that you meet with compliments and all these rampant, random communications, etc. but something gentle and nice like, "You know, that's a nice blouse." And they'll say "Thank you." And you'll say "I like it. Where'd you get it?" Pretty soon you will be engaged in conversation and that's a real indicator of a feminine quality.

MULTI-ANSWERS....YES!

That brings us to point number 4. When you answer a question, or somebody's talking to you, you're not going to answer with one word. Gone are the days. No more one word answers. It's not just "yes" or "no" all the time. You have to get into some "spirited language" that's going to actually drag you out of those simple one word answers. It's like this...

Woman: "Did you go to the movies last night?"

Man:"Yup."

The question is not really "Did you go to the movies last night?" The person asking, if she's a female, is asking about the movie. She wants to know if you liked the movie. She wants to know some piece of information about the movie. Would you recommend the movie? Who was in it? Anything that would kind of carry on and bring about conversation is almost really the viewpoint. Women enjoy this. It's a habit. It's like a creature habit. So that, one word answer... gone! Multi-answers... in!

ASKING A QUESTION

Women will ask questions like "Do you know what time it is?" and the pitch will go up at the end of the sentence. Men will say it more like a statement; "What time is it..." And so it cuts it off. It almost sounds accusatory "Yes, you know what time it is." The women will bring it up. Work on bringing your questions up at the end. Don't overdo it or you risk Valley Girl Phenomenon (VGP).

I just want to make sure that on the variation of pitch, you're not forgetting that questions go up at the end, as they should anyway, but the American culture has kind of worked us out of that behavior. This is the reminder!

FACIAL EXPRESSIONS AND GESTURES

There is so much information all over the place on this... where do I start. The word should be "subtle."

The entire body movement and facial expressions tend to be over-done. It can be to either side of the pendulum....too much or too little.

Often, when I'm walking through a city, say, San Francisco or Chicago, it is very easy for me to actually spot transgender and transsexual folks. They either appear to be in a catatonic state or overly zealous in the motions including walking or hair touching. Women do touch their hair....often. I touch my hair often. Many people touch their hair often. But it's done gently and it's done in passing. Women will hold their hands together, touch their face, check their make-up, rub their leg, but subtly. It is not just "sit still and be beautiful thing". It doesn't work that way.

You have to be relaxed and comfortable in your skin. Be relaxed and be confident in your minimal actions. This includes nice eye contact. The person with you knows you are paying attention. This is a very confident gesture.

A WOMAN'S TOUCH

Women like to touch upon meeting. We shake hands, give a hug or a simple touch on the back as a gesture of warmth and friendliness.

When you shake hands with women it varies, right? There's this gamut of handshakes from the "crunch", down to that little melty thing where their fingers just kind of like melt into your hand.

Some women just hug you right away. Women who hug you or kiss you right away, generally, have heard good things about you or have already been in communication some way, either by email, phone, work, whatever. "Oh I've heard about you!" and you just get the hug!

This "greeting touch" varies but generally, there is some form of a touch involved. So it's genuine to touch somebody's elbow or their hand in some gentle way that seems friendly and usual. And, if you genuinely have that affinity for that person, it's certainly a warm thing to do.

THE GESTURAL COMMUNICATION

The gestures, hmmmm, what is the right balance? I like to say that there is a balance to this; otherwise you can look like a circus act and potentially upset your listener.

Many people use or should I say, overuse, gestures and it actually becomes distracting in the communication. It can effectively change the nature of what is being imparted or received. For example, if someone is constantly raising her eyebrows during a conversation, this can be construed as disagreement or "*Reeeeally? Is that so?*" It appears to cast judgement on the speaker. So this added gesture definitely contributes emotion to the conversation, unintentionally or intentionally. It's the same with rolling your eyes. How do you feel if someone is rolling her eyes at you? You automatically feel a bit defensive to what you're saying.

Don't throw caution to the wind on these behaviors. Pay attention to your listener and have good eye contact. If you can maintain a friendly demeanor, even if you have a disagreement, it is more lady-like to wait until the end of the speaker's communication and then impart your opinion.

THE DIRECTION OF YOUR BODY

What in the heck am I talking about? I'll tell you...

When you are sitting with someone, typically it is a friendly gesture to shift your body toward her. The opposite of this would be to sit in a chair and have only your head turned to talk with them. There appears to be a higher interest in the person if your body is positioned toward them. A simple, yet powerful tip. This is also true for flirting!

You can usually see by the proximity of others, how comfortable they are with you. So, the more willing you are to share your space with them, the more interest they can see you have in them. Nice and easy! Please be able to observe the other person. If he looks comfortable, then ok, if not, back off! You will know soon enough if the interest is there.

WOMEN ORIGINATE COMMUNICATION

Women are "originators of communication" probably, (no definitely), above men.

Women typically walk into a party, and they're saying "Hiiiii, Hiiiiii!", while the boyfriend or spouse stands nearby hoping for a drink, trying to blend in. The women are right there letting you know that they've arrived and are happy to be there.

When you come to the house and the woman answers the door, she will welcome you, take your coat and offer you something to drink or eat. She will always want *you* to feel comfortable. It has to do with attitude.

Starting communication can be done in a variety of ways. It can be making a remark about an outfit. It can be a comment about the room or the environment. It can be about what was said on the news last night or some funny anecdote. It is always done to raise the comfort level of the company you're keeping.

THE COMFORT FACTOR

We're talking about a "comfort factor". Women are safe. Women are maternal. Women are daughters of people who look to their moms to make the cookies and create that smell in the house that says "home". There's a lot of comfort in women.

They have softer bodies and they have softer hair and they just have a softer disposition overall. They're not raring up to fight all the time. (At least most that I know aren't that way.) Women generally have warmness to them and a comfort to them. That's really part of the attitude.

When you communicate in any situation, a sporting event for somebody's child or a play you're going to or somebody's home for dinner or a holiday party or whatever it is, keep in mind this "comfort factor". If you are invited to a social event, bring something. "I brought the salad..." or ask what to bring or something of the sort. Understand that there is that communicative aspect to women. They want to bring comfort. They want to be friendly. They want to feel warm.

All of those characteristics and those traits, amongst the other things we've gone over already, are the things that really separate the male from the female in their voice and how they come across to others in life.

Always bear in mind that your own resolution to succeed is more important than any one thing.

~ Abraham Lincoln

THE QUALITY OF YOUR VOICE

This chapter has an additional tip you can incorporate after reviewing all of the previous information. I thought it might benefit you and give you a little bit more "hands on" when working on your own voice.

This is about "nasality" (nasal). Nasality has to do with how much of the sound comes through your nose when you phonate or talk. We talked earlier about how sound can come through your nose or come through your mouth. The point is, you want to have the best quality of sound that you can.

Therefore, I want you to be able to ***direct the sound mostly out of your mouth***. That's the point.

Here's a quick tip to identify whether you're directing the sound out of your mouth or it's coming too much through your nose.

When you say "aaaaah" you should be able to pinch your nose off and hear no difference in the sound. This sound contains no nasal quality. If the sound is all coming through your mouth, from your oral cavity, the "aaaaah" will not sound any different than before you squeezed your nose.

If it's coming through your nose, you will get a vibration that you can feel and the quality of the sound will change.

Thus, you can work at directing your air through your mouth. It's just a really quick tip to be able to identify whether you have too much sound from your nose or is it actually being directed from your mouth.

You want to sound the best that you can with your new voice.

So again, it's just "aaaah" (pinch nose) and that will let you know if you have too much nasality, too much sound coming through your nose, and you can work on redirecting it. And just by pinching, you can do it!

*For a successful technology, reality must take
precedence over public relations,
for Nature cannot be fooled.*

~ Richard Feynman

How To Feel Your Pitch

This is another chapter on helping you find your pitch. It's basically a **sensation** we're going to look for. We're going to use these three fingers (index, middle, and ring) and you're going to place them on that little notch in your neck as you're looking for your pitch. It will be a vertical position directly going over your larynx (Adam's apple). You have your octave, eight notes, and those are the notes that you can actually feel with your fingers, as your larynx moves up and down.

Now, when you get to the note you consider is a nice, easy comfortable note; higher up from your original voice, you physically can *feel* it. Maybe it moves up from your middle finger to your top finger or from the bottom finger to the middle finger or somewhere in between.

It's just another tool that you can use to monitor a physical sensation and work toward becoming your own coach. Place your fingers on your larynx, do your scale and feel the vibration of the correct note. Use this method and it's, "Oh yeah, I remember!"

You can even use four fingers if needed, or if you only need 2 fingers, that's fine as well. But just group them together and you'll be able to feel and you'll go "Oh there it is, right there".

So, place your fingers on your throat, establish the pitch you want, feel the sensation and vibrations on your fingers, note where on your fingers that note falls and remember it for later sessions.

Courageous risks are life giving, they help you grow,
make you brave and better than you think you are.

~ Joan L. Curcio

No Whispering

The important point of this chapter... **whispering is not good for your voice**. It's not good for your vocal folds.

Whispering occurs by bringing the vocal folds in proximity to one another. The folds are not actually touching. This is how you get the whisper quality.

The danger in whispering comes from the created high laryngeal tension and a very high flow rate of breath. This is why many people are "tired" from practicing their new voices. It's a forced, unnatural position on the anatomy and can cause damage over time.

Whispering is a "no no". Whispering is not something you should use continually or even try and develop this whispery or breathy kind of voice. It's just not ideal. The vocal folds are not made for that. You don't want to cause any abuse or misuse to your vocal folds by whispering and thus creating damage in that area. So don't do it!

A human being is only interesting if he's in contact with himself. I learned you have to trust yourself, be what you are, and do what you ought to do the way you should do it. You have got to discover you, what you do, and trust it.

~ Barbra Streisand

Let's Face It

This is the chapter on "confront". Every time you hear the word, confront, you may be thinking it's about fighting or confrontation or something you are coming up against. But in this case, I'm talking about how you face things. And regarding your transition particularly, I want you to be able to face everything you're coming up against, into, through, with ease and be comfortable at it and feel comfortable when you're doing it.

Life in general has a tendency to push your buttons and make you feel a certain way. Somebody gives you a look… you feel embarrassed. Or if somebody yells at you… you feel upset. Or if somebody ignores you that's also a communication that does something to you, to your mind, to how you're thinking. But it's really not you…those fears, those anxieties, those upsets, those things. Not to say you're not really experiencing them. We've all experienced those things. But it is not who *you* are. You are not your fear. You are not your "afraid", afraid to engage in, afraid to face, afraid to move into a new situation.

You are engaged in quite a big undertaking in your life at this point. And if you can recognize that there are buttons that are going to get pushed, by people, by friends, by co-workers, by all of those around you… walking through a parking lot, when you're mid transition, when you're mid-change before you've actually kind of put it all together, please realize that any uncomfortableness that you are feeling is **ONLY** some button getting pushed and/or activated. Ignore it, better yet, confront it and keep being who you really are.

In this book, with all the emphasis on voice work, your *attitude* is very much part of it all. The counseling, the surgeries, all of it is part of the package and there are buttons that are going to get pushed in each one of these situations. So, if you can raise your awareness and recognize that the responses from others really have no impact on *who you are*, then you will be in a good place. Those buttons can only give as much power as you allow.

Maintaining **yourself**, in attitude, is going to give you a much better position. You'll have more confidence; your awareness will be there. You'll actually gain an ability of being able to "be" in any situation comfortably and face it. And you can continue to do this in every location, in every situation and with every person. You look straight ahead, you look right at them and you just confront them and you feel good about yourself, even though your sweater got a hole in it during the day or coffee ran down your shirt. (You can even acknowledge, "Yes, I know, I have coffee on my shirt. Thank you for noticing.")

You know, if you're overt (up-front, in the open) and you're aware about the people around you, and you communicate about things, you're going to be less effected by your environment and more in control. So I want you to have the power to be able to do that. And tomorrow when you go out or go to the grocery store and you know the cashier's looking at you kind of "off" or she's just having a bad day or what have you… say something nice… a remark or compliment.

We talked earlier about compliments and manners and

niceties and building relationships with those people around you. It could really change anyone's day. It doesn't matter if you're in transition or not. We're *all* changing every day.

Decide not to be so affected by all of these environmental factors around you and keep your eye on the mountain. Move toward your goal and be able to withstand any kind of anything that's coming at you throughout a day. It really makes it easier.

I have a teenager, I have small children, and it's interesting in my life as well. I have different buttons than maybe you have right now. We all have them and they are around, but you can choose to let them affect you or you can choose to comfortably face whatever it is you come up against and continue to move on toward your goals, eventually reaching personal achievement and happiness.

Don't let anything stop you. You are worth it!!

*Life is just a mirror, and what you see out there,
you must first see inside of you.*

~ Wally 'Famous' Amos

OBSERVATION

I'm sure you're wondering why I'm writing about observation. We've done all this voice work and this confront thing and we're trying to be there comfortably and address all of these situations and make our home happy. But there's another part here which is....you have to be able to *see*.

We've talked so much about listening, using your ears and hearing. In addition to auditory coaching, one of your greatest powers is being able to see and look and notice. When you're out and about and you are observing things at the grocery store and you're looking at people, start to really observe what is in front of you. Take note. What is their appearance? What is their hair like? Is their hair pulled way up high on their head or is it low on their neck? What is their dress like? The way they walk? Their make-up?

You're doing it all of the time, this "observation thing" right? But what I really want you to take away from that, at least a piece of it right now, is, take a look and use those people as "Yes, that's a model, that's something I like to look at; that's something I'd like to look like."

Also remember however, you do have *your* body, *your* face shape, *your* hair color, and you have the usual things about you that do make up *you*. These are physical things in the material universe...even your body!

So while it's nice to look and want all of those other things, and want that hair and want that make-up and want that appearance... also look at yourself! Observe what you have and your characteristics and things that are actually attributes to you, because we all have them. We all have something unique about ourselves.

Use what you observe to help mold yourself and create what you want. Make sure you're developing yourself. *Your own style, your own "you", who you are* and not what's in the pages of the magazines with excessive, eccentric, looks all of the time. Something that's real for everyday life that you can live with that *others* also find pleasing to observe. Not the interruptive, double head turning, whooping run-way model type of thing.

Make it so that it's your style. You're seeing other people. Notice the image created. Maybe you can pick up a few things of how people hold their hands or shake hands or tilt their heads or touch their hair. Definitely observe all those things. But you don't want to pick up every single characteristic of every single person you're observing! You'll overwhelm yourself! You will make less of yourself thinking you'll never be able to do this. Certainly I admire and look at women and like certain outfits or certain ways they carry themselves but it's not necessarily something I can always adopt and take on as my own. I have to work within my own body...body shape...body size...hair color, thickness, appearance, whatever. (And yes, I realize all of the above can be purchased...for a small fortune!)

I don't want you to feel like you're up against a wall and you're not ever going to make that grade on the appearance or whatever. It really stems from your attitude and how you observe and what you do with your observation and how you can apply it to yourself so that you're actually making your own style with your own life. Ultimately creating the ideal **YOU!**

Fashion can be bought. Style one must possess.

~ Edna Woolman Chase

Appearance

There's only one chapter dedicated to "Appearance" and I will cover a few aspects of that subject.

MAKE -UP

One is make-up application. That information is so readily available to you on Google and on YouTube. You can look up videos. You can see how to apply your make-up... the smoky eye... 300 different ways! You can see the lipstick application and how it's done with brushes, liners, lipsticks and glosses. You can see how to apply foundation with the mineral make-up, powder and liquid based make-up. It's all readily available for you.

Make-up is fun and fun to create a look with. I'm not actually an expert in make-up application but I've done my own for years. I'm still trying to find the perfect mascara! But these videos are so professional and so easy to access. You can go to Cover Girl, Maybelline, Marie Claire, Revlon, Vogue... they have all of these application type sites that you can just click on and look for "eyes"...by color, by season by what's contemporary... night life, day life, all of it. So it's definitely, definitely an area where you'll find many experts and how-to's.

Number two, on the make-up...You can actually go into Bloomingdales, Macy's, or any of these high end stores, Niemen-Marcus, and they will sit you down at any of the counters, the Clinique counter, Estee Lauder, what have you, any of those brands and they will *do* your make-up for you. This is an up-side. They will let you try anything. You can put it on over and over, find the colors that match. Once you've done this you really don't have to keep going back again and again. That's a plus side.

The down side for me, personally, would be sitting in the middle of one of these big, department stores at the make-up counters while everybody's passing by and watching. That's not something I'd prefer. That's just a personal preference.

You can also look on-line. You can order things on-line and you can actually return them if you don't like the color or they don't actually work the way they said. All of these things do have that "return factor" and that's really nice. If you didn't know that you could return make-up, you absolutely can. You can even return make-up at Walgreen's! They will take it back if you don't like it.

Another thing, make-up usually does last a really long time. So, if you buy something, you're going to have it for several months. (Unless it's your favorite lipstick and you just keep using it over and over. Oh, and if it is your favorite and you are using it every day, then you should buy a few. Because chances are, they will probably stop making your favorite color, as they do mine, almost on an annual basis!!!)

Anyway, these are just a few things I have learned over the years as far as make-up goes. Like I said, you can always go on-line and find it. Demonstrations on how to apply it are on every website and every female magazine. Grab up some of the magazines. They'll have the addresses right in there.

HAIR

Next, hair, right? Hair is very different to every person...

the thickness, the color, the wave in it or the straightness of it.

If you're looking for a hair style that suits you, I would suggest going to a website where you can put in face shape and hair styles. Just Google that and you'll actually find a website that is going to come up and say something like "You have a round face? These are the hairstyles for you." That would make the most sense to optimize your new hair style and know what fits your face shape. If you have a pear shaped face, round face, oval face, heart shaped face, they'll recommend hairstyles that take the particular attribute that you have and make you the most attractive or the most beautiful regarding your hair. My friends and I have used this and it's really true. We all love it!

Now if you're not going to be using your own hair but are going to use wigs, make sure you get really high quality wigs. Get more than one, for sure. And remember, in addition to being glamorous, you'll want one of the wigs to be able to give you the "usual, everyday, blend-in, not over-the-top, not the night-life" kind of look. I know women love to be glamorous and I know we all enjoy buying shoes and heels and make-up and clothes and we all have more than we need and um... that's part of the fun of being a woman... because we have all these things we don't actually need! They are *just* for being beautiful. So, in addition to the gorgeous look, get a wig for everyday activities.

When you're trying out these wigs, you have to make sure that you're going to get a cut that is for you and that it suits your face shape. This can help you if you're trying to cover a jaw-line or if you have a small forehead or a large forehead etc. It's something to take into consideration. Should it have bangs? Should it not have bangs? Can it be colored or not or what are the up and down sides? How long will it last? Can I swim in it? What will happen to my natural hair in the cap if I do swim? Can it be washed? Does the color fade from the sun? Make sure you've checked all these things out. So that, you're not just doling out your money to get something that's not really the product you're after. And always, of course, ask for the return policy as well. I would recommend trying several types for comfort, fit and the customer service itself.

Let's not forget about extensions. What a brilliant solution! These are very nice and address several things about different types of hair and problems with hair.

First of all they are *real* hair. They are placed into areas of the scalp and completely blend in with your real hair. They are done in groups to thicken an area or they are individually placed. You can swim, shower and even where pony tails with them. They are as close to the real deal as you're going to get.

Hair extensions can be a bit pricy to start but then it is just the labor that needs to be kept up about every two months. Additionally, hair pieces can be attached and then hair extensions added. Magnificent! I'm practically selling myself on them!

They are gorgeous when done the right way. I have a contact here in California if anyone is interested. Send me an email and I will make sure you get a private consultation.

CLOTHING

I just want to mention a few things about clothing,

because it's really something that women struggle with altogether.

We all have different body types, shapes and so forth. You should know if you tend to go to higher end clothing stores, the sizes run smaller. So if you've been used to ordering something or buying clothes in a less expensive range, the sizes will be higher than the more expensive stores. Everybody likes to go from an 8 to a 6 or a 12 to a 10 or whatever. Just be aware of that. The lesser expensive clothing stores will be a certain size and the higher end stores, they tend to go down in size. And the fit differs depending on the brand, quality and designer. With some clothing, you kind of get what you pay for.

The other thing to mention about clothing is body shape. We all have different shapes. I mean, I don't think any woman I know is exactly pleased with the shape that they have and the clothing and all their fits and so forth. It is so different from shopping from a waist and length size in jeans to then looking at a size 10. You *HAVE* to try it on! You will see the variation in fit and style. Not all 10's were created equal. Some are cut straighter and some for a curvier shape.

One tip for you is that if you don't have an hour glass shape, you can try things like adding belts and/or accessories to change the over-all appearance of your body shape. A belt can kind of make you look like you have more of a waist than you actually do. If you have a "boxier" type build, belts can help. You could also try an "A-line" dress, which would be something that is tighter in the middle at the waist and it goes out like an "A". That is another method of helping you look like you have more of a shape as well.

If you really want to add some shape, you can also buy pads of any sort to enhance your figure. They can go in your shoulders. They can go in your boobs. They can go in your butt. So, if you're in a pre-surgery situation and/or you don't want to mess with certain body parts at all and you just want to kind of fill out some of the clothing so it looks smoother and has a better fit, you can purchase these pads. They are readily available. Stores like Victoria's Secret, Macy's, Nordstrom, all carry them. They will fill in your butt or your shoulders, and give you the shape you are actually looking for to fill your clothes in better.

Now, I'm happy to provide any feedback via in person, Skype or photos. I am used to doing that. My clients come over. They usually come with a bag of clothes and we're doing the thumbs up or thumbs down and it's a fashion show! I love to do this and find it fun! It is always nice to have a second set of eyes from a girlfriend.

The good news about clothing is that it's returnable including bathing suits, bras, and underwear. You'll either get store credit or you'll get your money back.

In summary for appearance, I suppose it's really about finding your own personal style. It's discovering what's going to make you happy and how you're going to live comfortably every day.

Every day is not about glam and suits and dresses and make-up and hair. It is about a baseball cap on a Saturday. Sometimes it's your favorite sweatshirt and sweat pants on the weekend or for working in the yard. It's wearing Ugg shoes that everybody seems to love and they keep your feet really warm. They are the comfort clothes and the relaxed style.

Of course, there are the days without make-up. I rock climb and I don't look like a fairy princess when I rock climb. I have the "do-rag" tied onto my head and I've got the weird shoes and there's nothing really glamorous about that at all. Your appearance should be used to manifest who you are and your attributes. Don't give up who you are for just an appearance.

Keep your confidence up and don't be embarrassed and everything will work out just fine.

A friend is someone who will help you move. A real friend is someone who will help you move a body.

~ Unknown

Movin' And Groovin'

HEELS

Those tricky, tricky heels! What can you do to improve that strut?

First of all, don't feel bad. It takes women loads of time to perfect their walk in heels. Just look around and see how uncertain many women look. The stilettos are not helping any of us, I'll tell you that!

Let' see if we can eliminate the obvious mistakes such as hunching, long strides, parted legs, lack of hip sway and confidence.

There are a few simple things to remember. First...no hunching. Stand up straight and with good posture. Practice this without heels and then with them. Keep your shoulders slightly back, tummy in but stay relaxed.

Heels are great and they make your legs look really nice! Anybody who owns a pair of heels knows this. They produce firm "muscle tone" in your legs and a bit in the butt! The nature of the heels themselves will make you feel a bit differently than you're used to. You'll get used to the sensation with practice.

Now when you start to walk, take shorter strides. This should naturally add a bit of hip sway. If not, pay attention and be aware that the heels will offset that feeling in your hips. They should slightly move with a sway.

Next, bring those legs in closer. You've seen the runway models walk with one foot passing right in front of the other. We're not going for runway style but when we're walking as women, we want to bring the feet to a point where the last step nearly was. If you take a look at the program I've done on-line, there are very nice demonstrations of this in heels and in flats.

I mentioned earlier about observing. Watch women in heels; the higher the heels, the shorter the strides.

When you're in a skirt or a dress you're more restricted in the hips and thigh area. You're not going to have the flexibility you're used to (unless you have a big, long, flowing kind of skirt or dress on). So, take shorter strides, keep your legs together, your hips will kind of naturally go back and forth. You don't have to emphasize that because it's going to happen just by the nature of wearing heels. If it doesn't, call me and we'll work on it!

FLATS

When you have your flats on, there's a little bit of a different feel. There's not much of a heel on most, if anything at all. There's just a little smidge of something so you don't ruin your shoes altogether. Anyway, they're really comfortable. They're really popular right now and almost everybody has them. You can wear them with a skirt. You can wear them with your pants but there's a little bit different feel. You don't have that heel bringing you up anymore. Keep your strides shorter, once again, so you're not doing some elongated, kind of ostrich step. The position is the same for the foot placement in flats as it is in heels.

CARS AND SKIRTS

Okay, another thing to think about and master is getting

in and out of a car. This is funny but it's something I see all the time. You have your bag and your purse and all your stuff, your groceries or whatever is with you at the time and you're shucking all this stuff in the car. Then it's this stretch to throw it all on the seat opposing the driver's and this "WOW"...all of your legs and girl stuff are showing! It's something that you have to pay attention to. Not ladylike!

When you have a skirt on, there's usually a slit in the back. It gives, but not *that* much. Make sure you've also snipped the thread that connects the slit; that helps!

Now, when you come to your car, open the door, take your bag and toss it across to the passenger seat, set it in the back seat or walk around to the other side and put your things in, but don't lean in and rail it across to the other side! Just give it a toss over. When you get in, face toward the open door. Don't face toward the rear of the car or the backseats. Now sit down on the seat with your legs *together*, kind of tucked in together and keep your feet on the ground. Now you can basically lift your feet into the car in a swivel motion....ta da! That's how you get into your car.

Alright, so hopefully that helped you with walking in heels, flats, posture and a little bit and with getting in and out of a car. The goal is really no more ripped skirts!

Politeness and consideration for others is like investing pennies and getting dollars back.

~Thomas Sowell

FEELING AT HOME

Let's talk about the atmosphere that you want to create in your home. It's a feeling of comfort and warmth. Unless, you're completely mean and have not one friend or family member who's speaking to you.

One of the things I've always noticed when I go to my mom's or my girlfriend's house, is the smell. There are candles burning or food that is cooking or some scent that you're used to smelling... some herbs in the kitchen or something's just been cleaned. These are all the things that when you walk into your home or anyone's home, you notice.

So as far as adjusting your body and your attitude, you should also be building an attitude and atmosphere in your home. For example, having throw pillows around, comfortable blankets for people to snuggle up with, the smell of herbs in the kitchen, or some fresh flowers out. You don't have to do this all the time but this is typically what a woman is providing; a feeling of warmth and comfort.

Martha Stewart, the queen of everything that she does and all the beauty and all the aesthetic value that she provides, are things that make you know that she is a woman, caring about her family, caring about her friends. Ok, the insider trading stuff, not too womanly, but you get the idea.

When you go to a woman's home there is always something offered. You know, there are a lot of manners and pleasantries, like, "Did you eat?" and "Do you want to sit down?" and "Would you like to take your shoes off?" It's just how most women create their homes.

I want to bring to your attention that your home is a reflection of you. So don't have vacant walls. Have artwork and pictures that represent you or the feeling of that space. Tell those who come in something about yourself by the way that you've decorated your home. Keep it neat and organized. You will feel good about it and so will others when they come.

If you're really looking to move ahead and do this whole transition fully, I just want you to have some attention on taking a look at your space, your home and what you're providing for others. Create an environment people feel they can come to.

You should represent *all* of you in every aspect of your life.

I want to prepare you and make you feel like you have a friend. And you do! Help is available and that's what I really want to impart. Your comfort, confidence and success are all very important to me. I want you to flourish in all areas of your life. Don't think for one minute you're on your own...you are not!

Fear is the cheapest room in the house. I would like to see you living in better conditions.

~ Hafiz of Persia

THE FIRST TIME

This is the final chapter and it has to do with **embarrassment**. But I'll tell you what...there are first times for so many things.

Remember the first time you rode a bike and you fell down or the first time you kissed somebody and you weren't sure if it was exactly right? Or the first time you went shopping and bought a bra or bought a top and cut your hair a different way? All of these "first time" things are memories that you can pay attention to or look at or hang on to. Or, you can just take a look and go, "This is the first time I'm actually revealing *who I am* and I'm going out with my new appearance and my new voice and my new attitude!" Now is the time you're actually revealing who you truly are *inside*. It is not just your appearance, your hair or your make-up.

Being embarrassed about stuff like, "Did my voice sound exactly right?" or "Did my hair look exactly right?" or "Was that the right outfit?" Here's a heads up...all women, all the time are concerned with this. This is not something that you would just be concerned with in transition.

And remember, the term "trans" itself means going from one point to another. You're moving through something to get to somewhere else. It's a journey. Guess what? These changes happen throughout our lives. From the time we're very small and can't walk and then we can walk and we want to run and then we run and then we want to drive a car... and all of these things occur throughout our lives.

This whole transition process, including the change of your appearance, the change your voice... is *temporary*. It's not something you're going to have to keep doing and reminding yourself about. You won't have to establish your hair style over and over. The laser surgeries and electrolysis will end for the hair removal. Your make-up only has to be purchased every so often. Fashion...what can I say???

So these points of embarrassment or being afraid to get out and use your voice or show off your new look are also only as embarrassing as you let them be. Let yourself off the hook and enjoy who you are. At any point you have the power within yourself to rise above these negative feelings. I'm with Nike on this...*"Just do it!"*

This is all about you and building your confidence through your voice and your attitude and keeping who you really are on the inside and out. You are not just an exterior shell. **You are who you are** and you're just trying to show this with your voice and your appearance and your clothing.

So don't let any of that hold you up. Go out, use your voice all of the time in conversation. Give it a go.

There's no need to back off from that. Just confront it and you'll be on the other side very soon!

Inspiration may be a form of superconsciousness
or perhaps of subconsciousness — I wouldn't know.
But I am sure it is the antithesis of self-consciousness.

~ Aaron Copland

SUMMARY

In summary, I want you to be happy, confident and most importantly, yourself. The tools in this book are for your use and practice to help develop your female voice and characteristics. If you find anything to be difficult or confusing, email me and I will be there for you.

You are a spiritual being, using your body to show who you really are.

The appearance is a manifestation of you as a *spirit*. If this is not true for you, take a look and see who decided to buy and read this book. Look at who makes the decisions in your life and who can impact the outcome. Look at your personal abilities and accomplishments. All of this amazing and fantastic ability comes from you...not your body. You will be able to accomplish anything that you set out to do.

I'm on your side. We're a team in developing and attaining who you truly want to become.

CONTACT INFORMATION

Lynette Nisbet is available for personal coaching. She'd be happy to see what your needs are so that you feel you can get exactly what you need.

Feel free to contact her at:
408-466-2054

lynette@myfemvoice.com

For more information on her instructional materials visit:
www.myfemvoice.com

CPSIA information can be obtained
at www.ICGtesting.com
Printed in the USA
LVHW111010010519
616223LV00001B/32/P

9 781611 700770